SAVING MY TEN

TAYLER HILL

FOLK&TALES

SAVING MY TEN

Contents

Dedication   vi

I   1

II   11

III   29

IV   39

V   52

VI   64

VII
Short Story   85

Resources   105
Acknowledgements   107

For my daughter,
If I had the chance to go back in time, I wouldn't change a single thing.

-Mom

LOVING YOU HAS BEEN MY LIFE'S GREATEST PRIVLEDGE

I

Teen Births statistics state that in 2018, there were 6.3 births for every 1,000 adolescent females ages 15-19 or 6,932 babies born to females in this age group. Births to teens ages 15-19 accounted for 1.8% of all births in 2018.

I did not beat the statistics. I am the 1.8.

> One centimetre of dilation or a cheerio for visual representation. At this point, you are in early labour. The cervix is beginning to dilate and thin, getting ready for baby to make its way into the world.

> How exciting. Or is it? I was seventeen. Perhaps excited wasn't the right word. But what would be the right word?

> Petrified? Terror-stricken? Those are synonyms for scared; perhaps those words will suffice.

For now.

Physical pain 1/10

Emotional pain 2/10

I give my physical pain a one because I know I have to save my ten. If I show my cards and give a ten already, there would be no way I'd make it through the next 48 hours. My emotional pain gets a two because there was no point in my pregnancy where I wasn't in some state of melancholia.

It was a brisk February, and I was due in four days on the 12th, exactly nine months after my birthday, a gift I didn't expect to receive for my seventeenth.

Where was I going four days before my due date? I was getting my eyelashes done, and I was excited, hence the two on my emotional scale. I even got to drive there myself since I had just gotten my license. Let me say that again; I had JUST gotten my license; I could have sex and be trusted with another human's life, yet I couldn't drive a car up until a month ago. It's funny when you think of it from that perspective.

I was also excused from classes, one of the few perks of being pregnant in High School. It turns out you get out of exams when you have a baby; I wish I had known that sooner; I would have had a baby before my grade 10 science exam.

Excuse my dark humour; if I don't laugh, I cry.

My belly button was numb as I scraped off my glacial-coated car; my coat no longer zipped. I saved my pennies during those nine months. I let my leggings dig into my hip, and my shirts stretch beyond their capability. I figured if my body had to do it, perhaps my shirts wouldn't mind either. Besides, new clothes aren't in the budget when you have nine months of working a part-time minimum wage job to try and save for the next 18 years.

I don't know why I felt the need to have lash extensions before birth; who was I trying to look good for? My nearsighted newborn, who the world was fuzzy to? Perhaps I thought I'd try my luck at picking up a man in the maternity ward. Or rather, for an Instagram picture, to fabricate the reality that I had just pushed a 7lb 5.oz baby out of my who-ha and was injected with pain meds into my spine. No, can't show human fallibility. I wanted to in-still the image of "Look how put together I am; I'm going to be the best Mom ever!" Oh, to not be controlled by the influence of others' crass thoughts, but alas, I'm a Gen Z, and social media ruined me.

I was pretty uncomfortable at my lash appointment, but not much more than I typically was on a regular day, being on the brink of birth. I even went for sushi with my Mom after (no raw fish, of course). Why did I add that in here? I don't know you, and you don't know me, but here's a not-so-secret secret about being a teen mom. So many people expect you to be a lousy mother, and so many people are rooting for your failure that even at 23, over five years later, I'm still trying to prove myself a good enough Mother to everyone. Even to you, stranger. So please note I treated my body as a temple while pregnant because, apparently, I need you to know that so I can sleep at night.

I'm tragically human; forgive me.

I couldn't sleep later that night. Even though the Braxton hicks were becoming scarcely real, it still wouldn't click that I was in labour. I think I knew deep down if I let it be true, everything would become too real. At that moment, I was the *single* pregnant teen; I was afraid to become the *single* teen Mom. Most of all, I was afraid to pass my pain along with my genes onto her. The ache of abandonment would no longer be only my burden to bear but hers too. I could justify myself; everyone in my life had given up on me at some point, but not her. She deserved better. Better than You and better than me too.

After nine months of fearing and longing for this moment, it was finally here. As my one slowly increased to two, I knew I was in labour.

11

Two to three centimetres dilated. At this point, your cervix is stretching from the size of a penny to the diameter of a banana.

Physical pain 5/10

Emotional pain 8/10

I would like to say I was exhausted after a long sleepless night of contractions, but I was naive to think that that was exhaustion. I would soon learn the true meaning of the word.

I am still saving my ten. I will need that later. I'm sure of it.

I had a doctor's appointment on the morning of the 9th. My Dad drove me. I would have driven myself, but the pain was too consuming for a rookie driver.

I waited for my name to be called while gripping the rickety plastic chair in silence as each contraction rose and fell, too ashamed to show my pain. But it didn't matter; I was too focused on my embarrassment rather than the straining cramps. I hoped so badly no one thought my Dad was "with me with me." I should have just been thankful that I wasn't alone, like most of my pregnancy, like the rest of the appointments I had been to.

> You should have driven me. You should be the one here next to me. It takes two to make a baby, but only one has to walk around with the evidence, the responsibility.
>
> Fair? Has there ever been such a thing in this world?

The nurses joked as I walked in. "Any baby yet?"

To their surprise, I responded, "Actually, yes."

They were so excited. I was glad someone was. I desperately wanted to be, like a normal person would have, but you can't be a normal person when you're stuck in an abnormal situation.

> I put myself on autopilot and set it to *survive*. Each day blended into the next, a small piece of me withering away with the days. A dark cloud formed around my head and I soon forgot what it was like to live without it hurting, to breathe without being angry that it wasn't my last breath.

I wanted to be excited. I really did. But I couldn't, not without You.

I had to tell You that the baby was coming. I knew You would freak out, but I figured You would want to know when the combination of *us* makes her grand entrance.

I sat in the passenger seat, heated seats on blast to ease the contractions slowly working their way up to full force.

I texted you.

"Are you sitting down?"

"Yeah, why?"

"I was just at the doctor's, I am 2cm dilated, and they said she would probably be here tonight or tomorrow. Please don't freak out."

"I won't."

You did.

I went home and had a hot shower. Not in the hopes of easing my contracting body but for superficial reasons. I twitched and lurched as I struggled to blow dry and style my hair between the waves of pain. I shuddered as I applied my foundation and too much mascara as the waves kept growing and growing, crashing down on my cervix until I could no longer fight the hurricane developing inside of me. I retreated to my bed in hopes of shelter and comfort, but you can't run away from a storm that's inside of you.

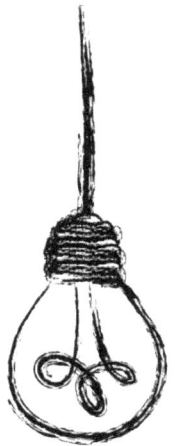

I STARED AT MY CEILING

AND FOUND A TINY SPEC ABOVE

I named that my focal point. They say when you give birth to find one, something to stare at to get you through the throes. A teddy bear, a picture frame, but for me, a spec. At least, that's what Google said. All I knew about giving birth came from the World Wide Web. I desperately wanted to do birthing classes, but shame and loneliness overruled and convinced me not to go. Anyway, I figured if women in third-world countries could triumphantly take on birth unmedicated in mud huts, I, too, could survive.

Hopefully.

> Nearly 24 hours since the first contraction, my body begged no more, but with each wave, it roused me awake, reminding me who was in control, then letting go and taking bit by bit a piece of my strength along with it. How much more did I have to surrender to this monster called pain?

I texted You again, squeezing my phone, contracting between messages until the blood curdled to the tips of my fingers, turning them pallid white.

"It hurts so bad."

"I'm sorry."

"I can't take it anymore."

"I'm sorry."

"I wish you were here."

"I'm sorry."

What were you sorry for? Sorry for the pain? Sorry for getting me pregnant? Sorry for abandoning me when I needed you most after four years together? There was a lot to be sorry for.

But I was sorry too.
Sorry I chose You.

Timing your own contractions is hard.

The physical pain was nothing compared to the ache in my heart. I yearned for You. At one point, I swallowed my pride and even begged You, but all I got was a shameful "I'm sorry, I can't." I thought all those nights I silently screamed and salted my pillow was rock bottom, but I think this was it. Never again would I beg for a man.

Lesson learned.

I've barricaded my heart, wrapped a chastity belt around it, and thrown away the key. This heart has already had its lifetime of anguish.

No more.

Please.

I often wonder about the toll my pregnancy had on others, like my parents. I hid my pregnancy for six months, refusing to take off my winter coat despite the beads of sweat on my brow. I hid my secret for so long that it only gave them a small window to go through the five stages of grief before coming to terms with the fact that their child was having a child.

I remember some hagged lady criticizing my Dad, blaming him for my teen pregnancy because he left me alone with a horny boy. Imagine that. Had she never been a teenager before? Stopping teenagers from having sex is about as likely as a triple rainbow.

I hope he never blamed himself. I hope the thought of that never kept him up at night, but I bet it did.

...

> My Dad sat on the stairs outside my bedroom door. He was worried about his little girl. I'm sorry, Dad, your little girl left long ago. She stopped being a child the minute the strip turned pink.

Darkness took over the day, as it was approaching 9:00 pm on the 9th. I was in labour for 32 hours and counting. I spent hours rocking back and forth on my knees with my head buried between my elbows and my sheets balled into my fists. Hours turning my heating pad to the highest possible setting, hoping it would malfunction and scorch my cramps. Hours of trying to find comfort within the pain. At this point, I didn't care what my app told me; it was time to go to the hospital and get the damn epidural.

Nine steps up the stairs felt like I was summiting Mount Everest, but after five minutes and multiple breaks, I made it to the top. Small victories. It took another ten minutes to put on my thermal boots and winter coat as my body succumbed and crumpled to the pain. After hours of pain endured and my contractions minutes apart, I figured she had to be close.

After a short yet lengthy car ride, we arrived at the hospital. My Dad dropped me off outside of emerge; Dad says hospital parking is a scam.

I was supplied with a wheelchair ride up to the delivery ward by a horrifically chatty young man, who I'd be happy to talk to if I wasn't about to push a bowling ball out of a keyhole. I nodded and fabricated a smile as he communicated his amazement at my reticent's. If only the bewilderment rendered him speechless.

> Sir, if you grew up in my household, you would have known that pain and suffering are one's own battle, not to be presented to the public.

Hospital rooms are so depressing. The lifeless walls, the incessant **beep beep beep**, death lurking around every corner. You'd think after a long day of fighting your way out of your Mom's vagina, you'd at least see a pretty rainbow or unicorn painted on the wall.

I wriggled my way into a pale blue hospital gown and dragged myself onto a weathered bed to be checked for dilation progression. The bloodproof sheets crinkled under my weight and echoed through the room, amplifying my loneliness.

The nurse came, and I spread my legs, waiting for the good news. Since my check-up at 9:00 am, over twelve hours ago, I dilated a total of 1cm, which brought me to a whopping 3cm dilated. If my body hadn't been so fatigued, I would have punched the wall.

I texted You. Again.

"I'm at the hospital."

"ok."

"Are you going to come?"

(...)

III

Four to five centimetres dilated. At this point, your cervix is stretching from the size of a Ritz cracker to a Babybel cheese.

Physicals pain 7/10

Emotional pain 6/10

My parents advocated for me because I could no longer do it for myself. They knew I wanted You. No. Needed You. I couldn't conjure a pleading message through the incessant cramping, so they did it for me. No matter how hard I tried, I could not summon You here. Not even a shooting star or a genie in a bottle could make that happen.

I no longer believe in miracles.

Nurses and needles and needles and nurses.

Poke. Ow. Poke. Ow. Poke. Ow!

"Sorry, I can't seem to find your vein for the IV," the nurse said with a furrowed brow.

No kidding.

"We're so sorry; there's only one anesthesiologist in the building right now. You will have to wait another half an hour," the nurse apologized.

I am so sick of sorries. When is it time for me to be on the other side of the sorry? The grass seems greener over there. But I'm a people pleaser, so instead, I smiled and said, "I have been labouring for nearly two days; what's another half an hour?"

Time moves slowly when you're watching the clock.

I kicked my parents out of the room. Although it was nice to see the divorcees unite for the occasion and reconcile over their daughters' pain, I still didn't want them there. I only wanted You, and if I couldn't have You, then no one would do. No one could or would suffice.

>Just You.

>But where were You?

>Barricaded in your room, I would later learn.

I battled for another half an hour, aching for the needle to plunge into my spine and grant me some relief. This was a big statement and attestation to the pain from someone who used to have four nurses pin them down for a flu shot.

A flow of nurses circulated in and out of the room like a revolving door. Checking charts, changing bags, looking between my legs, *repeat*. Every time the door opened, I shot up, fingers crossed, hoping the one person I yearned for would be walking through the door.

You.

I survived the half an hour, counting down the minutes with the clock. A new nurse came in, steadying a petite needle in one hand and my IV in the other. "We're so sorry," she said, "it's going to be another hour and a half, but we're going to give you some of *this* to help with the pain."

She injected a small vial of liquid into my IV. The *"some of this"* was fentanyl. Wasn't that the drug everyone was overdosing on? Wasn't that the drug on the news that they warned us about? Why would they give this to my baby and me? Shouldn't they have asked? Many good questions. It wouldn't have been the first time my opinion had been dismissed by healthcare because of my youth. How could I know my body or what I wanted when I didn't even know to use a condom? Apparently, the two coincide. Stupid then stupid now stupid always, I guess.

I was on cloud nine. My limbs fell to my side, liberated and free from the pain; my body had never felt so detached. That was until the next sharp contraction rolled around. I still felt everything, except now I was drugged, and my body was limp. So fighting took more, everything was felt more, the drugs stole my strength, and if I didn't have that, what did I have left? Perhaps that half-eaten Wendy's spicy chicken sandwich from a day and a half ago would kick in and save the day.

I jammed my eyes shut, hoping to escape the pain. Like a child who curls their toes into the comforter away from the monster under their bed.
Naive.

> But the pain found me, of course. You can't play hide and seek with yourself.

I felt the second most remarkable thing in my life that day, your hand reaching for mine.

Miracle

noun

A surprising and welcome event that is not explicable by natural or scientific laws and is therefore considered to be the work of a divine agency.

IV

Six to seven centimetres dilated. At this point, your cervix is stretching from the size of a chocolate chip cookie to an orange slice.

Physical pain 8/10

Emotional pain 4/10

I don't know if it was guilt or force that brought you here; I didn't care. You were here in the flesh and not just a figment of my imagination.

That's all that mattered.

It was kind of like a group project when one person does all the work, and the other one misses everything, but you're just thankful they showed up for the presentation.

Exactly like that, actually.

> Perhaps I will give miracles another chance because this sure felt like one.

As our fingers intertwined, a surge of strength that I so desperately needed shot through my body. I opened my eyes, but I didn't need to; I knew it was you. I knew the back of your hand better than my own. The grooves of your knuckles, the indents on your palms, and the soft scent of ivory across your skin. For the first time in nearly nine months, I breathed.

You sat at the edge of my bed, clasping my frail clammy hand in your sturdy one, only letting go to wipe it clean on your high school football hoodie. I remember when you got that hoodie, you told me I couldn't steal it like the rest, but we both knew that was an empty threat.

I liked your sweaters. I liked how they swallowed me and hung down to my knees. I liked how they smelled like you and felt like home. I liked how they weren't your sweaters, but ours. I remember you throwing them to me as I shivered on the sidelines, cheering you on at your games. I remember how the girls were flooded with jealousy as I trotted around with your number on my back. I remember how we were known as the high school sweethearts, inseparable since grade 9, never to be torn apart. All of that was true, until I got pregnant.

Until my stomach became her sweater, a fleshy cocoon she calls her first home. Until I looked forward and saw myself being more than the girl on the sidelines, but the Mother of the star player. The Mother whose relationship never wavers with her daughter, but flourishes with each passing day. The Mother who's sweaters she will steal because they smell like me and feel like home. The Mother-Daughter duo, never to be torn apart.

I look forward to keeping my promise to her, a promise to love her and stand by her no matter what.

A promise you failed to keep for me.

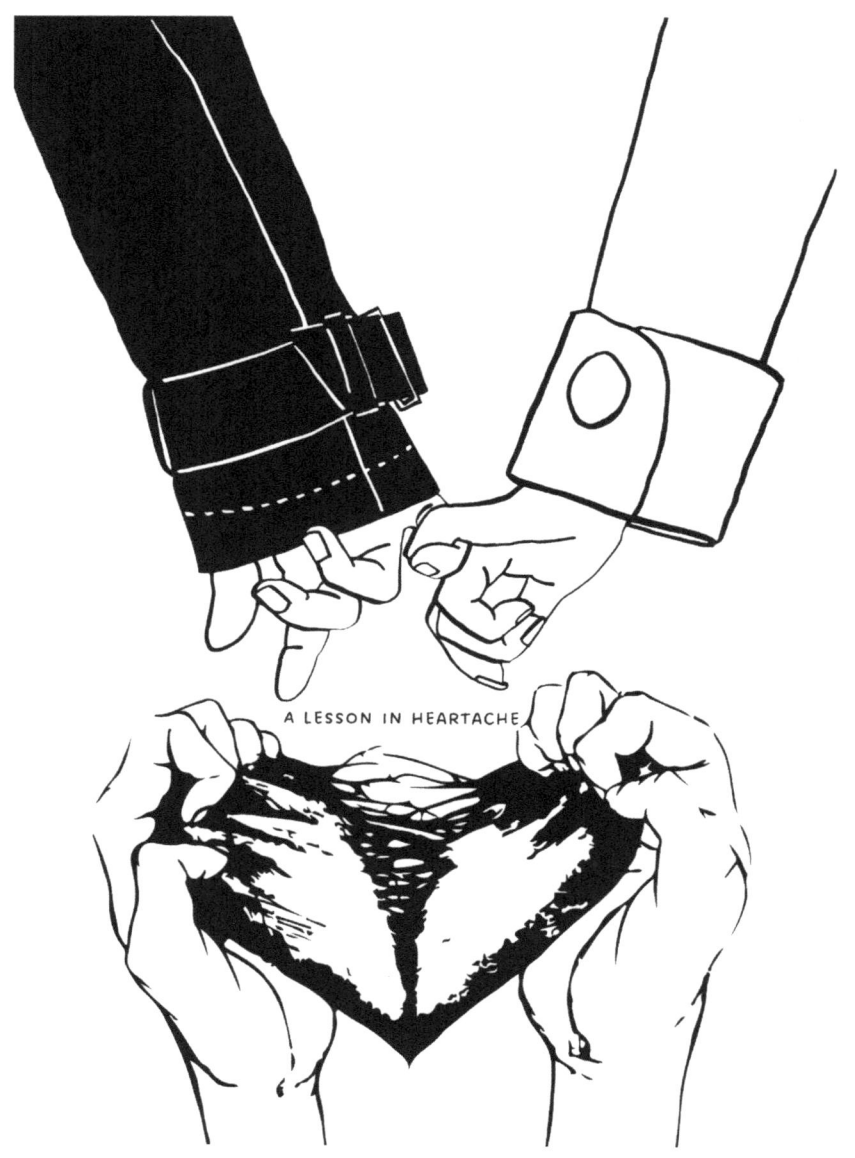

Each time You let go of my hand, I scrambled for it back, desperately on the verge of a panic attack. I didn't realize the magnitude of how much my body longed for yours until I couldn't have it anymore. I'd never experienced this kind of **fear**, the kind that embeds itself in your flesh and bones. The **fear** of losing someone you had already lost before. But as your hand came back to mine, I once again was safe, until you let go again, and the **fear** came rushing back.

The nurse escorted You out for the epidural procedure.

A white-haired man entered. The man with the drugs. He might have been God, but maybe that was the fentanyl talking. Regardless, he was my lord and saviour. He had a face that ventured many trips around the sun. He had the kind of sternness that would be used to train Russian spies. I was nervous, but then he called me sweetheart, and I felt safe. I cherished names like that, like when You used to call me baby. But then You stopped, and baby became a forbidden word. One that made your heart thump and palms sweat. It was an unspoken agreement not to utter the word. So we removed it from our vocabulary. If we didn't say it out loud, the word couldn't hold any weight.

I knew I was in good hands despite one of his holding a three-inch needle readying itself to sink into my spine. He talked to me like a human being and treated me with care. The nurse that had been there since I was admitted held me steady, her maternal arms linking around me while the white-haired man talked softly while injecting me with the sweet-sweet syrup.

Relief.

In the movies, the wife drapes her arms around her husband's neck while he cocoons around her body, holding her steady while she flinches and seizes as the needle descends into her spine. *In the movies*, he whispers sweet nothing to her, words of encouragement and praise. *In the movies*, the man is part of the birth. He suits up in baby blue scrubs and cuts the umbilical cord through teary eyes. *In the movies*, he's grasping the woman's hands, supporting her while looking at her with undeniable bewilderment in her strength and love in his eyes.

I wanted that look. I still do.

I used to grimace at the pain in the movies, but now I am flooded with the ugliest emotion, **jealousy**. But one thing they don't tell you about the movies is that life is nothing like them, and if it were, mine would be categorized as an epic tragedy.

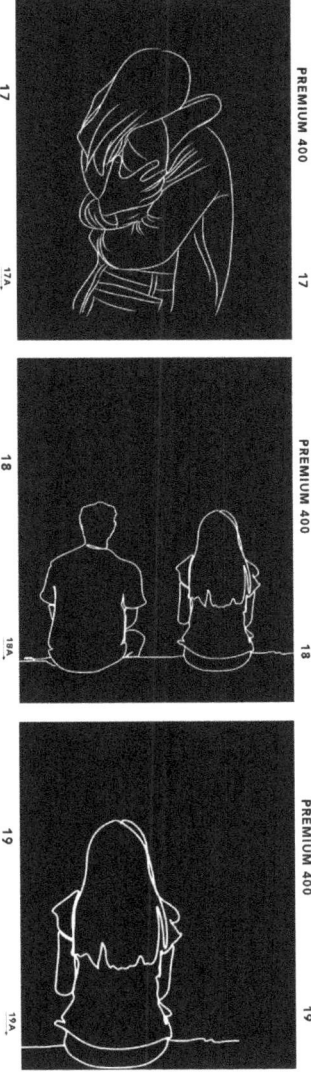

V

Eight to nine centimetres dilated. At this point, your cervix is stretching from the size of an apple to a doughnut.

Physical pain 1/10

Emotional pain 6/10

The lady in the room next door was screaming. She was a no-epidural hippie or whatever you wanna call it. I call these women crunchy Moms or anti-Tylenol Moms. The kinds that take their kids with fevers of 104 to chiropractors. I wanted to walk over there and tell her about the magical syrup that takes all your pain away, but I had lost total feeling in my legs.

> The epidural worked well, too well, I would soon learn.

After a few more cervix checkups, the nurse came in and broke my water; another reality check for me. I thought I would be strutting down Broadway in my pea coat during the first snowfall of the season when all of a sudden, my water breaks dramatically while the side character (the ugly fat friend) rushes me to the hospital while I frantically call my husband, who happens to be in the most important business meeting of his life. I need to stop watching movies. I don't live in New York City, nor did I have a husband, and all three of my friends (not ugly or fat) were probably hanging out in a Tim Hortons parking lot. But hey, I did have a pea coat.

It was a weird sensation; the epidural numbed me from the waist down, but I could still feel the strange goop leak out of me and surge down my legs. It reminded me of how I ended up here in the first place.

I rested on the hospital bed, as gleeful as a half-paralyzed person could be. I shifted toward you, careful not to falter my gown and expose my belly and scare you away. I wanted to talk, but You told me to get some rest, but how could I? There was so much to talk about, so much to say. We had been apart for nearly nine months, and finally, we were together... Right?

"Is your favourite colour still orange?"

"Have you watched the new season of Stranger Things?"

"Are you going to stick around for us after I give birth?"

Some questions you want the answers to so badly that you don't want to hear them.

During my entire pregnancy, I asked You the golden question: "Are you going to stick around?"

To which I would always receive an answer that somehow danced and limboed around both yes and no. I teetered for months, not knowing if I was going to keep the baby. I came to the conclusion that if I wanted to keep her, I would first need to accept the terrifying possibility of doing it alone.

And I did. I accepted with a heavy heart.

You feel like a new person when you are pain-free. The birds sing louder; the sun shines brighter, heck I bet if you asked me to do a triathlon, I would have said, "hell yeah!" (Not really, but you get the point).

You urged me to get some much-needed rest, so instead, I Facetimed my sister. I told her it was okay that she couldn't be here, but I could still hear her heart breaking through the screen. One of the most difficult parts of my pregnancy was keeping a secret from the person I shared everything with. When I finally gained the courage to tell her, I could physically feel some of the weight lift off my shoulders. I can now see now how foolish I was trying to tackle something that was so much bigger than myself.

Regardless of how badly I wanted her by my side, I refused her three-hour drive from Kingston on this particularly snowy winter's night. One life was coming into the world; I didn't want one going out. Plus, she was a terrible driver on a good day; mix that with snow and midnight, and that makes a recipe for disaster.

I told her not to worry that lots of people were probably in the waiting room, and one less person would ease the chaos. I was wrong. The waiting room was nothing but crickets between two long-ago lovers. Your parents, sisters, friends, nobody but my parents showed up and waited anxiously for their first grandchild. The way it should be. There was a lot of should-be's that never happened.

I was once asked by an old friend expecting a child who was seeking advice on how I managed to make sure no one was in the room with me. I said, "Darling, I didn't have a choice; all I got was a text saying:

"I'll stop by if we have time."

As if cruising by to meet your son's daughter was like stopping in to try a piece of cherry pie.

It's been a long journey toward this moment. I remember holding my small baby bump early on in my pregnancy with tears streaming down my cheek, apologizing to this little thing that would not become anything. I apologized and told her that I had to abort her; if I didn't, I'd lose him.

"Can't you understand?" I pleaded to the floating fetus in my uterus. "I don't want to lose him." but I didn't want to lose her either.

"Oh god," I cried; "why did I put myself into this situation?"

It's much easier to pile the blame on yourself than on the person you love. It's hard to take off the rose-coloured glasses when you've lost someone.

I sobbed as I begged for her forgiveness and told her that maybe one day we would meet each other, how I hoped so badly we would.

I've come a long way since then. We both have.

I took a nap, a well-deserved nap, no more than an hour or two. I could have slept for hours peacefully, pain-free, but the nurse came in, and to her surprise and mine, I was ten centimetres dilated.

It's time.

IT TAKES A STRONG PERSON TO TRANSFORM FEAR INTO POWER

VI

Ten centimetres dilated. At this point your cervix has dilated to the size of a cantaloupe and is ready for birth.

Physical pain 9/10

Emotional pain 9/10

I had anticipated and feared this moment for nine months, and it was finally here. So, of course, when the nurse told me I was ten centimetres dilated, I said what any rational person would say,

"Can I have ten more minutes, please?"

Oh, cmon, It was 4:00 am, and I had been in labour for nearly 48 hours; at this point, I think ten more minutes wasn't too selfish to ask for.

I pushed for a few minutes while You stood statue-like above my shoulders, looking everywhere in the room, but "down there." I struggled to push with no feeling below my waist, but I was more concerned with Your discomfort. I asked you if you would like to go and you did.

> Don't ask questions that you don't want the answer to.

I hoped you would pull through at the end, but as the steel door closed behind you, so did my faith in miracles. Even though I was only seventeen, I had been dreaming about this moment my whole life. Call me naive, but I loved You. And what is the pinnacle of love if not you and the person you love most mixed into one?

I dreamed about it, all of it. You holding my hand as I push, You cutting the umbilical cord, You kissing my sweaty forehead while our baby lays on my heaving chest. I didn't get any of that, and I never will. You don't get a second chance at a first experience.

> You jumped into my dream and made it a nightmare.
>
> A piece of me died that day, and I am still mourning the loss.

The nurse leaned between my legs and told me when to push. I tried and tried, but it's hard to bare down and follow the pressure when your vagina is numb.

After half an hour, her heartbeat started to rise, and I became the priority birth on the floor. The doctor came in, carrying a strange steal contraption that looked strangely like salad tongs. I'm glad I never researched what forceps are or what they do, and I suggest if you plan to give birth, you refrain from further research as well because if I knew, I would have been dragging my numb legs off the bed and out the door.

I heard a bunch of medical terms that I didn't know the meaning of, such as **Fetal Tachyarrhythmia**. I knew that words with that many syllables never mean anything good.

Something snapped inside me, a primal mother-like instinct. Some force within found the strength I needed to push. I had to get her out, and my body knew exactly what to do.

I had never screamed like I did when the forceps entered my canal and stretched me beyond ten centimetres. I told the nurse I was going to throw up, so she grabbed me a bowl unphased as if this was a normal reaction to the pain.

I threw my hand up to grasp onto Yours, but you weren't there; I was grabbing air.

"She's beginning to crown, " the doctor said, steadying his hands.

The room was busy with doctors and nurses and specialists, I was a stranger in my own room. I had no one. I didn't feel comfortable with Mom and Dad there, we didn't have that kind of relationship. And You left. But She was there, the nurse who came in shortly after I was admitted. My angel in scrubs. I remember when I saw her, heart on her sleeve. She wore a smock, tattered and beryl and her chestnut locks secured under a cap. Dark bags lined her under her eyes as she entered in the dead of night for her third half-day shift this week. She took Your part and did it gracefully, filling the dead air with words of encouragement. She put out a hand when the pain was no longer bearable while she tied my hair and held the bucket, taking moments to look between my knees, probably wondering why I wasn't taught the bird and the bees. The last moment of my nine-month nightmare was near its end, and there she was, making it a happy beginning. She wore a smock, tattered and beryl, but it should have been wings and a halo.

I hit 9 on the 10 scale, still wanting to save my 10, but what was I saving it for? I was in the home stretch, I could use it. But I didn't feel compelled to.

I bellowed, "I can't do this!" as I squeezed my own hand while I pushed. The pain and adrenaline peaked and came flooding out as she did.

February 10th, 2018, at 5:42 am, after nearly 48 hours of labour, she made her arrival.

I did it.

I waited to hear a thunderous cry as they pulled her out of me. My heart sunk to my feet as I waited the endless three seconds for the sound of survival to roar out of her and know she was okay. It's music to your ears once you hear the beautiful serenade of the wail.

As they placed the gummy baby covered in my own blood and guts onto my chest, I was elated. I became flooded with fear and love and happiness and anxiety and joy and every emotion you could possibly feel I felt in that moment.

> She was finally here. Welcome to the world, my love.

All along, I had been saving my 10, so scared to hit it, afraid that I wouldn't recover. Little did I know, I had already hit it.

> Finding out the gender alone was a 10
> Going to every ultrasound alone was a 10
> Crying hysterically in my bedroom every night was a 10
> Hiding my pregnancy for six months was a 10
> Isolation was a 10
> Shame was a 10
> Loneliness was a 10
> Missing out was a 10
> Heartbreak was a 10
> Giving birth without You by my side was a 10

I feared ten, and I loathed ten; little did I know I survived ten and a lot of them at that. I was a walking survivor of heartbreak; now it was time to take the remnants and build myself up again. It was time for a new start.

I gave you my last name because he didn't deserve his legacy to be carried on through you.

I did.

I AM A LOTUS

    I HAVE CYCLED THROUGH LIFE AND DEATH

AND I AM IN MY

  MOMENT

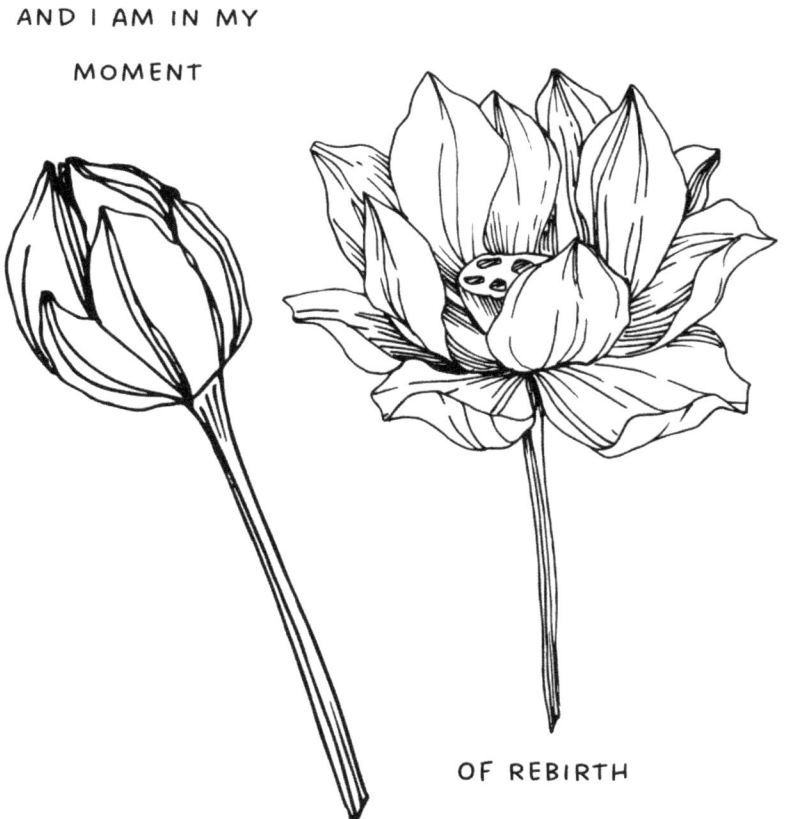

    OF REBIRTH

It was finally the calm after the storm.

After a 48-hour long labour, there was one thing I wanted when the nurse asked me,

"Can I get you water or juice?"

Despite the rose-pink light of dawn signifying the birth of a new day, I responded to the nurse,

"Got any ginger ale?"

To which she responded with a nod and a smile. Perhaps my drink of choice at such an early time in the day exposes my adolescence. I slurped back my drink as if my life depended on it, absorbing the comfort of the ginger, the dancing of fizz on my tongue, and the soothing crunch of ice between my teeth. For a brief moment, the world stood still, and I forgot that I was seventeen, now responsible for a whole life. I forgot about my duties, having to guide this little soul through life. After hours of my body contracting, I brought my daughter into the world, squeezing my own hand as I pushed. I had anticipated and dreaded this moment for months, and here I was, surviving in the aftermath.

I relished my pop, not noticing the nameless nurse whose twelve-hour shift was over; she left as swiftly as she came. I never got to thank her for filling Your spot. I never got to thank her for being my person when I had no one. But most of all, I never got to thank her for restoring my faith in miracles.

I indulged and basked in the triumph of what my body could do. I immersed myself in the glory of how truly exquisite a woman's body is and each warrior mark left behind striped across my once smooth skin. What was once a round tummy now looked like a deflated balloon. In a body I felt so unfamiliar in and did not recognize as my own, I thanked it for the marvellous thing it bestowed upon me.

I deserved my favourite drink, and it did not disappoint. The cooling liquid soothed my burning throat from the hours of screaming at the top of my lungs. The bursts of bubbles waltzed on my tongue and down my throat, filling the room with colour. The pale depressing walls were now crowded with bounties of blues, pinks, and yellows. A space that felt like death was now full of life. My daughter's life.

As I indulged in the wonders of ginger ale, it was like a toast to myself. Here's to taking on the challenges of motherhood, here's to new beginnings, but most of all, here's to us. I was drinking away my sorrows of the past and leaving them behind me while welcoming my new life with open arms.

The lavish taste was taking away my aching body and aching heart with each gulp, making me stronger until the dreadful moment of the last sip. I shook the flimsy plastic cup aching for every last drop in fear that without it, I would become weak again. I looked over at my baby girl, empty cup in hand, and heart as full as could be when I realized I would never have to be alone again.

I feared becoming the *single* teen mom, but there was nothing single about me. It was me and you now. I would forever be plural. I would no longer have to stand in the loneliness of being singular or depend on a man to take me out of that state. I did it myself, and I finally felt at home on my own with you. Together.

Plural: *more than one.*

To my sweet Jade,

It is an honour to be your Mom.

You saved my life, and I don't mean that figuratively; you, my dear, are the reason life is worth living, you are my tether to this world. I never knew how wildly and deeply I could love someone until I met you. I never knew what it was like to give every part of myself to someone until I met you. I never knew what home felt like until I met you. Everything I didn't think I could be, I became because of you. Once, I only dreamed of becoming this person, and you gave me the ability to do it, a reason to work for it.

My entire life has been spent in survival mode. Always thinking what's next, how to keep moving forward, but you remind me to slow down, to experience. You are sunshine, and what a privilege it is to bask in your light. I am your mother, but you are much more to me than a daughter. You are a friend, you are a soulmate, you are you and what a divine thing it is for me to get the chance to love you, to live in this lifetime with you as your Mother, your guide, your biggest supporter. Our stars aligned when we were placed on this earth at the same time. I promise to look for you in every lifetime.

Loving you has been my life's greatest privilege.

-Mom

I hit my 10 again, except this time on a new scale.
The happy scale.

VII

Short Story

Ten Minutes

On particularly lonely nights, when dusk has long fallen, and all that can be heard is the rhythmic sound of a cricket rubbing the edge of its wing against the other, creating a noise to taunt and amplify my loneliness, are the nights my thoughts consume me. It's the nights like these I spiral down memory lane and think of my younger self. Particularly my seventeen-year-old self, fresh out of labour.

As the dishes go unwashed and the laundry piles up, I gaze at my five-year-old nestled into my thigh, sound asleep; her honeysuckle curls splayed across my lap. I brush a strand away and indulge in her ever-changing face and grant myself the privilege of closing my eyes for *ten minutes*.

February 10th, 2018.
9:38 pm.

I open my eyes, and I'm in a hospital. I frantically walk up and down the hallways, looking for signs to direct me to the maternity ward. I move with purpose, knowing the sensitivity of time. I hate hospitals. There's something about breathing in air embodied with sanitizer and death that makes me feel uneasy, but I refuse to be distracted; I'm on a mission.

It's unsettling how quiet it is aside from the sharp beeps and the subtle flow of oxygen through tubes; I try my best to make my steps feather-light, careful not to wake the dead and dying.

I struggle to find my way through the maze of yellowed halls and fading fluorescents; it's been so long since I was here last. Everything looks the same, right down to the icy steel bedpans and neon needle disposal.

I interrupt two nurses in the middle of a heated conversation over who's taking out the old man's catheter in the room down the hall.

"Excuse me, do you know where the new maternity ward is located?" I huff.

They point down the hall and brush me off as a nuisance.

I pick up my pace. Time is of the essence. Tick, tick, tick. I arrive at room 304 and look at my watch...

9 minutes and 38 seconds left.

As I walk into the room, six beds are lined adjacent to the wall—three on the left and three on the right. Thin blue curtains act as walls, sectioning the beds off into cubicles. Only one is in use until tomorrow morning when an entitled lady fresh out of a cesarean takes it upon herself to calm the room with whale noises. Luckily, I won't be here long enough for that.

I make a sharp right and peer through the fabric barrier. There's a young girl, no more than seventeen, sullen in a blanched hospital bed. A newborn lay adjacent to her in a clear plastic cubby padded with cotton foam only arm's length away. This part of the hospital is much nicer than the other. Depressing still, but at least she has a TV.

I step out from behind the curtain and clear my throat to make my presence known.
She looks up at me, eyes rimmed red and puffy. She begins to sit up but winces from the pain.

"Stop," I urge her. "You need to rest."

She begins to open her mouth.

"You don't have to say anything," I whisper.

I gently place my hand on the sound-asleep newborn swaddled in milky white muslin. I want to pick her up and cradle her in my arms for 9 minutes, but I'm not here for the baby. I'm here for the girl.

I ease towards her as I would a frightened fawn. Slow movements and my hands stretched out front to show that I come in peace. When I sit on the edge of her bed, the silence is broken by the crinkling of the plastic sheet. I lean forward and cup her face into my hands. I gently graze the tips of my fingers over her warm flushed cheeks, stained blush pink like a peony. She lets me stay in this moment with her. Her eyelids are heavy and twitching with exhaustion from the 48-hour labour she just endured. She shuts her eyes, and I let out a sigh of relief; she trusts me, and she knows she is safe with me. Her eyes are closed, but tears still fall, streaming down her cheeks along my forearm and pooling down at the crease between my elbow and bicep. We sit here like this for a moment, tears streaming from both our faces. I shift slightly, angling myself closer to her. I'm careful so that my movements won't disturb the blood proof sheets and risk waking the baby. I press my forehead against hers, letting our tears collide together, creating a mixture of sadness, relief, exhaustion, longing, and happiness.

"I don't have long," I say, "I only have...."
8 minutes and 46 seconds left

As I pull back, I can't help but study her face. The contour on her cheekbones, the too many swipes of mascara, the tutti fruity lip gloss smeared across her lips, I can't help but feel like I'm looking at a stranger. But we are bonded, if not on the outside, on the in. I feel a connection, a power surge of emotions fusing us together. An umbilical cord connecting her and me. A storybook in which we are both the main character. She is me, and I am her, but something separates us. She's so young; she's so fucking young. So much younger than I remember, so much younger than I felt.

An unsettling feeling plants itself into the pit of my stomach and spreads its roots into my veins. I don't know what it is—this unfamiliar familiarity.

It must be her youth, her blind adolescence. Her body looks untouched, virgin-esqe. If she didn't have a baby next to her, I would have believed she was pure. To imagine her spreading her legs and doing the unspeakable is an untouchable thought. The same feeling you get when you watch porn for the first time; you want to look away but can't.

I study her for a bit longer. As I'm taking in her fountain of youth, I can't help but feel sadness shift inside my heart. She still needed her innocence protected. She had barely dipped her toes in the ocean of life, and here she was, having created one.

I snap myself out of it. I have to. I know time is sensitive, but I don't know where to begin. The words get jumbled up in my brain and come out like word vomit. A mix of "ands" "ors" "so's," and other conjunctions with nowhere to go. There's so much to say I don't know where to start first. I look her in the eyes and hold her stare for a moment. She's waiting for me to say something, something profound and meaningful, something life-changing, something to take away her pain, but I can't help but struggle looking into those toasted brown eyes, wanting more than I can give.

As soon as I start, I can't stop it from pouring out.

"I have thought about this moment numerous times over the past five years. I pondered what I would say if I were ever given a chance to speak to you, but now that the time has come, I feel at a loss for words. I know you're scared. Everything has changed, and the weight of the world has come crashing down on you. Everything feels so much more real than it did when she was in your belly. You are responsible for life now; preserving it, nourishing it, being everything you never had and more, which is terrifying, to say the least. The fear of failure is terrifying, but don't look at it as a bad thing; use it as fuel to keep going even when you feel burnt out." I scratch the back of my head in hopes of itching out something more profound to say other than my shred of lacklustre advice.

"From this moment on, everything changes. And I'm not saying this to scare you; that is the last thing I want." I pause so she can hear the sincerity in my voice. I need her to know I mean no harm; she's had enough.

I continue, "You will have to work harder than you have ever worked. You are going to have to sacrifice a lot: your body, your mind, your life, everything. You will watch your friends move on and live completely different lives. They will travel down paths very different from the path you are headed now, but I think you already know this. I know you already know this. And I didn't come here to lecture you, although I think I may have already failed at that part. I want you to be ready, not to be blindsided by your life turning upside down."

Her eyes hallow back into her head, and I know my words

haven't done justice; they've done the opposite. I search my brain for more to say and redeem myself when the baby starts to stir and coo. I watch as her motherly instincts already kick in. I am so proud of her. She struggles to sit up, shuddering as the pain of her stitched-up wound bleeds with each movement.

"Do you mind?" I ask.

She nods cautiously.

I gently scoop the baby in my arms, making sure to cradle the bum and support the neck. My hands tremble; I forget how to hold a baby; it's been so long.
After a few seconds, instinct kicks in, and it becomes natural, as if no time has passed. Even if your mind forgets how to Mother, your body never does.

She watches me as I hold her baby, taking notes. As I kiss the baby's hands, I marvel over each finger; they are much smaller than I remember.
I lay my love all over, letting her know I'm present. Mamas here. The touch of my lips on her skin always does the trick. She's already relaxed, like she's back in the womb. I sway back and forth like ocean waves kissing the shore, receding, and coming back again. I follow the flutter of her eyelids until she is back to sleep. Before I put her down, I bring the nape of her neck close to my nose and inhale the new baby smell; freshly baked bread, Mama's milk, with a hint of floral from the soap. I don't want to let this breath go; I want to hold onto this smell forever. Exhaling feels like a goodbye, and I'm not ready for that. I don't think I ever will be.

I gently put the sleeping baby back in her bin and look at my watch...

7 minutes and 40 seconds left.

I turn back to the girl and continue my speech. "You are going to experience the saddest sad and the lowest low you could ever imagine."

I pause to let that sink in for a moment, watching the fear of her fate submerge into her. I interrupt before my words hit her heart.

"But," I begin," "It is all worth it."

She arches her brow, studying me like I've lost my mind.

I begin to explain, "The love that that little girl will bring you is immeasurable. It is like nothing you have ever experienced. It's not the kind of love you can buy or get from a lover or a friend. It is unique. If magic were a feeling, it would be this." I'm fumbling for words; I know what I'm saying isn't doing justice. How does one describe love? It's like explaining a rainbow to a blind person.

The corners of her mouth turn up slightly, but I can tell what I've said isn't enough, so I keep going. "How can I put this? You sacrifice your life, your body, your food, your sanity, yourself, everything, but it still doesn't feel like it's enough. The power of love is overwhelming. You will give that baby every part of yourself and still search for more to give because they give you the greatest gift of all. They give you–"

"But wait," she interrupts, "Is her Dad in her life? Do we get him back?" She looks at me with pleading eyes, begging me to give her the answer she wants to hear.

I brush a piece of stray hair out of her face and tuck it behind her pierced ear. I feel like I'm about to tell a child Santa isn't real.

"Listen..." I start, but she has already slumped her shoulders in disappointment and checked out of the conversation. "Hey, hey," I say, trying to grab her attention back. "I didn't say no; I just didn't come here to talk about him. I don't have the time. Do you see him here right now? No. I'm not here for him; I'm here for you and that little girl over there," I say, tilting my head to the right.

She nods, but her fists are still clenched.

I look at my watch...
6 minutes and 26 seconds left

She sits with her knees together and bum pushed back so that the weight centre's on her tailbone to ease the pressure off her stitches. Streaks of dried blood speckled with afterbirth permeate across her chest and down her middle finger; she looks like she's gone through war. And won.

Between her legs, I can see the extra large pad sticking out from her blood-stained postpartum panties. Despite changing her pad every half an hour to catch the never-ending flow, she still manages to bleed through them. On her arm, a purplish sore swells from where the nurse stabbed and struggled to insert the IV into her weakened pulse. I feel sick, bile shifting its way up my esophagus as I watch her sitting in her filth with no one here to help her.

"Look, I don't have long here, but would you like to take a shower? I bet some warm water would feel good." I try not to make it sound forced, I don't want to hurt her feelings, but I also don't think I need to state the obvious.

Her ears prick up at the word shower. I help her out of bed and sling her arm without the bruise around my shoulder so that I can take the brunt of the weight. I fiddle through her hospital bag; I know exactly where everything is; as if I packed it just the other day. I turn on the shower, making sure to check the temp periodically. Not too hot, not too cold. I remember how painful heat is when it scorches your raw, swollen breasts.

As I'm arranging the travel-size shampoo and conditioner, I can see her in the corner of my eye, naked and vulnerable. She's looking at her reflection, poking at her once round and smooth belly, now deflated and streaked with angry red tiger stripes. A belly that once was full of life is now lifeless. She can't understand why she feels so empty when she should feel so full, but she doesn't dare say that out loud. She can't grasp being in a body so foreign and unfamiliar, a body she doesn't recognize as her own. I watch as she traces her fingers along the deeply rooted marks, tears forming at the cusp of her eyes.

She turns her face towards me and meets my gaze. "These go away, right?"

I don't have the heart to tell her. "Come on, darling," I say, reaching for her hand to pull her away from the self-loathing, "The shower is ready for you."

As she eases in, I take a moment to look at my watch....
5 minutes and 12 seconds left

I walk around the bed's perimeter toward where the baby is sleeping. On her cubby reads "Baby Girl Hill." I giggle softly, only a tiny draft of air releasing from my nose. She doesn't have a name yet and won't for another three days. But the one she picks is worth the wait.

I gently trace my fingers along the baby's eyebrows and down her button nose; I'm making sure to take mental notes and photos of her markings. The way her lips form the perfect cupid's bow—the birthmark on her forehead from scratching my pelvis on the way out. A picture could never suffice this beauty. She is the eighth wonder of the world.

I don't want to rush her out of the shower, but I don't have much time left. There's something I need to tell her.

I bite my tongue and hold out for another 30 seconds. I spend each moment in silence, watching the baby's diaphragm rise and fall with each breath. It's like watching your first sunrise and last sunset.

When I hear the knob of the shower squeak and shut off, I stand abruptly and head for the bathroom, towel in hand.

I look at my watch...
3 minutes and 4 seconds left

"Why didn't you come earlier? Like when I was in labour. I could have used someone; I think I broke that nurse's hand," she giggles. I'm glad she hasn't forgotten how to laugh.

"I thought about it," I reply while patting her down with the over-washed starchy towel. "I know how lonely you feel in this big quiet room, so I thought you would appreciate some company."

She nods, ashamed that I know how empty she feels right now, how much the guilt is eating at her. Why should she feel so lonely when her baby is finally here? Shouldn't this be the fullest she's ever felt? I wish I could take that feeling away from her, to let her know that she is a great Mom and it is okay to feel your feelings rather than shove them down. But I know her too well; every bad thing she bottles and every compliment she gets goes right over her head.

I slide the hospital gown over her head and lace the back into a bow. I feel guilty for not being able to get her a fresh one that doesn't have her blood stained into it, but my time is running out; I have to do what I came here for, but she has so many questions.

She sits back on the bed, struggling to find comfort within the pain.

"How old is our daughter now?" She asks.

I smile, "She just turned five."

"What's she like?" She questions.

"Well, she's our daughter, so obviously super cool," I say, emphasizing the sarcasm at the end. I don't want to reveal too much; I want her to enjoy the journey and the bitter-sweetness of watching our child grow up.

"What about-"She starts, but I hold up my palm to cut her off.

"I'm sorry; I know you have a lot of questions, but I can't answer much; I don't have long" I frown.

I check my watch...
1 minute and 22 seconds left

I start to panic, time is cutting close, and I haven't done what I came here to do yet; I hope I haven't lost my chance.

"I know you are so scared for what's to come and what the future holds, and you have every right to be. You are taking on a massive responsibility, and at such a young age, at that." I feel like a broken record of all the adults in her life telling her everything she already knows.

When I try again, I'm interrupted by a thunderous wail erupting from the baby. A hunger cry, something she could only help to console. My palms dampen with panic as the clock ticks with each second that goes by. I scratch at the over-picked hangnails on my thumb, something I always do when I'm stressed. I don't have time for this, but I would never dare say that. I may have lost my chance.

In the midst of my panic and over-picking, I come to an abrupt halt when the corner of my eye catches and witnesses something life changing. While I was consumed in my mania, a bell was ringing in her head, a call to *motherhood*. She sprung into action, putting her pain second to the baby's needs. She struggled as she tried to recall the extensive research she did on articles titled *Breastfeeding 101* or *Breast Feeding as a New Mom* or *Breastfeeding for Dummies*. She points her tender nipple into the baby's mouth and flinches as the baby latches to her rawness. Tears begin to stream down my face, and I beam with pride. My stress is overruled by a new feeling, *relief*.

She is going to be okay.

I wipe away my tears before she notices and take a deep breath. I organize my thoughts and words and know exactly what to say, something that I wish someone had told me.

"Despite the difficulty, despite the mountains you have yet to climb, it is all going to be worth it. Do you know why? Because that little girl loves you. When she looks at you, whether you are all dolled up or just woke up, her face will light up no matter what. Most relationships in life are formed based on what people can get from you, money, sex, and status, but not her; not that little girl. She loves you because you are you. It is the purest form of love you will ever experience in your entire life. And you know what you have to do to earn that love? Exist. That's quite remarkable, isn't it?"

I don't need an answer; I can see it in her eyes and smile.

I continue, "If you ever find yourself in a position where you are lost and questioning what's this all for? What is the point of all this? All you have to do is look down at your little girl because all the answers you will ever need are right there.

I look at my watch...
10 seconds left

"I have to go; I'm sorry."

I lean over and plant a gentle kiss on her and the baby's forehead, and make my way to the door.

As the door begins to shut behind me, I plant my foot at the bottom and hold it open; I have one more thing to say. I turn around and ask, "Can I tell you something? Honestly?"

Her brows furrow and a touch of worry sets in. "Yeah?" She says hesitantly.

"I love you, and I am so proud of you."

Resources

Teen Pregnancy Resources

If you or someone you know is struggling with teen pregnancy, please refer to the resources below or contact your local planned parenthood.

Note: These resources are Canadian Based.

Wellness Together-
CALL 1-888-668-6810 or text WELLNESS to 686868 for youth

Kids Help Phone- 24/7 mental health support:
CALL 1-800-668-6868

Massey Centre-
CALL (416-425-6348)

Jessie's: The June Callwood Centre for Women and Families-
CALL (416-365-1888)

Humewood House-
CALL (416-651-5657)

Acknowledgements

Wow, where to begin?

First off, I would like to thank You. It has always been my dream to become a writer, and I wouldn't have been able to do that without your support. So, from the bottom of my heart, thank you.

I would also like to thank my family. I know what you went through during my pregnancy wasn't easy for you either, but you were still there for me when I was in my darkest place, when I needed you most. For that, I am eternally grateful. I would also like to thank my close friends, Zoe and Haley, who stuck by my side throughout my pregnancy and into motherhood. I hope everyone in their lives is lucky enough to have friends as amazing as you guys.
Another big thank you to my peer support. Gabrielle Goudie, Ashley Haynes, and Arianna Zangara. I have been working on this book for five years, and if it wasn't for them, I wouldn't have been able to make this book into something I am proud of. Through their edits and encouragement, I was able to turn my work into the best version of itself. Thank you so much, ladies.

I would also like to thank and recognize my daughter's Dad. We have come a long way together. From two scared teens to young adults raising our sweet girl. You may not have been there in the start, but you have been there every day since, loving her alongside me. So, thank you. Thank you for supporting my writing, and thank you for giving me the greatest gift of all, our daughter.

And last but certainly not least, my daughter Jade. Thank you for being my inspiration. Thank you for your love. And most of all, thank you for choosing me to be your Mom.

I love you.

About Me

Hello! i am

Tayler Hill

Tayler Hill, a Canadian author hailing from the vibrant city of Toronto, Ontario, brings a unique blend of passion and expertise to the world of literature.

Instagram: @taylerhillauthor

Tiktok: @folkandtalespress

Find me on socials

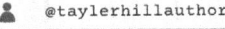 @taylerhillauthor

Copyright © 2023 by Tayler Hill

All rights reserved. No part of this book may be reproduced in any manner whatsoever without written permission except in the case of brief quotations embodied in critical articles and reviews.

First Printing, 2023

www.ingramcontent.com/pod-product-compliance
Lightning Source LLC
Chambersburg PA
CBHW052114200426
43209CB00076B/1957/J